Careers

Samantha Taylor | How to get ahead in

Beauty

www.raintreepublishers.co.uk

Visit our website to find out more information about **Raintree** books.

To order:

☎ Phone 44 (0) 1865 888113

🖹 Send a fax to 44 (0) 1865 314091

🖥 Visit the Raintree bookshop at **www.raintreepublishers.co.uk** to browse our catalogue and order online.

First published in Great Britain by Raintree, Halley Court, Jordan Hill, Oxford OX2 8EJ, part of Harcourt Education. Raintree is a registered trademark of Harcourt Education Ltd.

© Harcourt Education Ltd 2007
The moral right of the proprietor has been asserted.

Editorial: Melanie Waldron and Lucy Beevor
Design: David Poole and Calcium
Illustrations: Geoff Ward
Picture Research: Melissa Allison and Fiona Orbell
Production: Huseyin Sami

Originated by Chroma Graphics
Printed and bound in China by South China Printing Company

10 digit ISBN 1 406 20442 0
13 digit ISBN 978 1 406 20442 1

11 10 09 08 07
10 9 8 7 6 5 4 3 2 1

British Library Cataloguing in Publication Data
Taylor, Samantha
Beauty. – (How to get ahead in)
646.7'2'02341
A full catalogue record for this book is available from the British Library.

Acknowledgements
The author would like to thank the following:
Thanks to Oonagh, my tutor at Hastings College, for inspiring me all those years ago! Also my thanks to all those who contributed their ideas and help in gathering the information needed, including HABIA. Also to Jamie Lloyd who swiftly replied to all my emails when I needed information on personal training and fitness.

The publishers would like to thank the following for permission to reproduce photographs: Alamy pp. 5 (A. Parada), 31 (ACE STOCK LIMITED), 7, 36 (BananaStock), 26 (Brand X Pictures), 6 (Design Pics Inc), 21 (Doug Steley), 37 (Roger Bamber); Corbis p. 44; Corbis pp. 32 (Helen King), 23 (zefa/Frank Bodenmueller), 48 (zefa/Helga Winkler); Getty Images pp. 22 (Digital Vision), 35 (ImageBank), 29, 38 (Photodisc); Harcourt Education Ltd p. 19; Harcourt Education Ltd pp. 43, 49 (Tudor Photography), 9, 11, 20, 27 (Gareth Boden), KPT Power Photos p. 25, TIPS Images pp. 15 (Chad Ehlers), 13 (Mauricio Polverelli), 4 (Steven Walthew), Virgin Airways p. 17.

Cover photograph of golden make-up reproduced with permission of Corbis/ Royalty-Free.

Contents

Words appearing in the text in bold, **like this**, are explained in the glossary.

If you wonder what a career in the beauty industry is all about, then read on. It isn't just about putting on make-up! There are many different careers to choose from – you could work as a therapist, hairdresser, make-up artist, nail technician, or personal trainer. The most difficult choice is where and how to train, and deciding on the career path to take.

What other careers can offer you the chance to travel, have fun, meet exciting people, and do something you love, while also helping others to feel good about themselves? From working in a salon to being your own boss to cruising the seas, the beauty industry can offer you all this and the chance to progress to management level with a top salary to match!

The beauty industry

The beauty industry covers several different areas of work, which are summarized on page 5. Various jobs are available in each area. This book looks at these career paths in more detail, to help you choose the direction you want to go in.

Get ahead!

As with any career, you have to work hard if you want to be the best. However, you can train in hair or beauty by learning on the job or taking qualifications that link directly with the job that you are going to do.

left: *This make-up artist applies dramatic stage make-up.*

Beauty in the United Kingdom is thought of as the best in the world due to the excellent training available. You could work on cruise liners or in health spas throughout the world. You may even want to **specialize** in a particular area such as **aromatherapy** or **electrolysis**.

- Hairdressing is an industry worth over £2 billion each year, and successful hairdressers can take their pick from many top jobs.

- Make-up is a very competitive business and you have to be prepared to work hard. You could be a make-up artist for film or television, or work on photoshoots for magazines.

above: *As a hairdresser you could be working anywhere! This hairdresser gives a demonstration to a packed audience.*

- Nail technicians create the perfect talons, either natural or fake! They are in demand everywhere, from high street nail bars to television and magazine work.

- Fitness instructors concentrate on creating the best possible body for people, by training muscles, improving posture, and increasing fitness.

- Health and **holistic** therapists cover a wide range of **complimentary therapies** such as **reflexology**, aromatherapy, and massage.

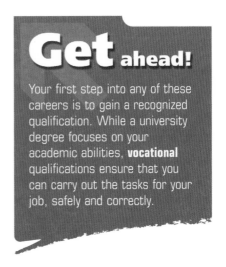

Get ahead!

Your first step into any of these careers is to gain a recognized qualification. While a university degree focuses on your academic abilities, **vocational** qualifications ensure that you can carry out the tasks for your job, safely and correctly.

Chapter 1

What is it all about?

There are many different jobs in the beauty industry. Each one involves different skills and training. Within each job there is also the opportunity to specialize in different areas, depending on what interests you the most.

Types of jobs available

Hairdressers

Hairdressers work with clients of all ages, cutting and styling their hair. They use techniques such as blow-drying, colouring, and perming. Some salons specialize in particular styles and clients, for example, Afro-Caribbean hairdressing, colouring, perming, or barber services for men.

Hairdressing can be physically hard as you will be standing all day. You could find yourself working in a salon or a cruise liner, or working as a mobile hairdresser visiting clients in their own homes. There are also opportunities for **freelance** hairdressers to work in film and television.

There are no minimum qualifications to begin training – it is more about having the right attitude and personality. You can train full-time at college or complete an **apprenticeship**. This usually involves going to school or college 1 day a week, then training in a salon the rest of the week.

Get ahead!

Recognized hairdressing qualifications include:
- NVQ/SVQ Levels 1–3 in Hairdressing
- **City and Guilds** Level 1 Certificate in Salon Services.

left: *This stylist adds highlights to a client's hair.*

Promotion is available for the right people. Alternatively, you may prefer to continue training and move into the fields of colour enhancement, wigmaking, or **tricology**.

National Vocational Qualifications (NVQs) or **Scottish Vocational Qualifications** (SVQs) are available in Hairdressing at Levels 1–3. Trainee hairdressers are qualified to NVQ/SVQ Level 1 and will help with shampooing and drying customers' hair, reception duties, and sorting towels and gowns. You will also sweep up, clean up, and make drinks – you are there to help the stylists.

Beauty salon assistant

As a beauty salon assistant you will be expected to:

◎ help therapists with their treatments
◎ set up and clear away treatment areas
◎ carry out reception duties such as making appointments, doing product displays, greeting clients, and offering them **hospitality**.

With experience, you may eventually carry out treatments on clients yourself such as **manicures**, make-up, and basic facials.

Get ahead!

Recognized beauty salon assistant qualifications include:
• City and Guilds Level 1 Certificate in Salon Services
• NVQ/SVQ Level 1 in Beauty Therapy.
These qualifications can be completed at school during Years 10 and 11 (1 day a week) or at college. If you want to progress further it is then possible to study for a Level 2 qualification to become a beautician.

below: *As a beauty salon assistant, part of your job will be to welcome clients and make them feel at ease.*

Beautician

To become a beautician you need to train for 1 or 2 years to achieve Level 2. Once qualified, you will be able to carry out treatments such as manicures, **pedicures**, make-up, waxing, facial treatments, brow shaping, lash perming, and lash tinting. You will also complete units for health and safety, teamwork, and promoting goods and sales.

If you want to progress further it is then possible to study for a Level 3 qualification to become a beauty therapist. This qualification will give you more options in your career and a better chance of promotion and travel.

Beauty therapist

To become a beauty therapist you need to be qualified to Level 3 standard so that you can carry out treatments such as electrolysis, body massage, electrical facials, and body treatments or holistic therapies, advanced nail techniques, heat treatments, tanning, and specialized make-up.

Beauty therapists often complete a full-time course for 1 or 2 years before training in specialist areas. This can include Level 4 qualifications in salon management or complementary therapy such as aromatherapy, reflexology, Indian head massage, **Reiki**, stress management, and electrolysis.

Get ahead!

Qualifications to achieve Levels 2 and 3 include:
- NVQ/SVQ Levels 2 and 3 in Beauty Therapy
- NVQ/SVQ Levels 2 and 3 in Spa Therapy
- BTEC National **Diploma**
- **Vocational Training Charitable Trust** (VTCT) awards
- Vocational Awards International (IHBC, IIHHT)
- International Therapy Examination Council (ITEC) awards.

APPRENTICESHIPS

Apprenticeships are available for students wanting to work and study in hair or beauty therapy. A training wage is paid by the employer and the student usually goes to college 1 day a week.

Salon manager

You will be qualified to Level 3 or 4 with either a business and management qualification or a lot of experience working in the industry as a senior therapist or stylist. You will be expected to organize staff **rotas**, training, **stock**-taking and ordering, wages, banking, accounts, advertising, and marketing. Your hours will be long – you will usually be the first one in and the last to leave at the end of a very busy day.

Make-up artists

As a make-up artist you will apply make-up and possibly style hair for television, film, or stage performers and presenters. You will be expected to carry out research to find out about the different designs, hairstyles, and costumes that the make-up will need to compliment. You may also do period make-up (relating to a particular historical period) and **prosthetics**.

above: *Make-up artists can spend hours working on prosthetic make-up.*

Working hours are long and you must be prepared to work at unusual times. Some work will be outdoors on location and may involve overnight stays. Make-up artists often need to carry a lot of equipment.

You will usually start by completing a hair and beauty or make-up qualification. Competition for jobs is fierce – you will need to be good at your job and very dedicated. You will also need to be available during filming to touch up make-up and tidy hair.

◎ NVQ/SVQ Levels 2 or 3 Beauty Therapy (make-up route)
◎ FT2 (Film and Television Freelance Training) specialist courses – New Entrant Technical Training Programme for make-up/hair assistant
◎ London College of Fashion (LCF) – Diplomas in Image Styling for Performance and Hair and Make-up Styling
◎ Foundation and BA (Hons) degrees in Specialist Make-up
◎ BA (Hons) degrees in Costume, Technical Effects, and Make-up for the Performing Arts.

Magazine/session stylist

You will need to be qualified as a beauty therapist or hairdresser, or be in fashion – or maybe all three! Your job will be to style models for photoshoots so they look fantastic in magazine photographs. This will include dressing, **accessorizing**, and doing hair and make-up. Artistic flair and attention to detail is a must. Your job will involve lots of travelling to and from studios for photoshoots, so you must be organized and always on time, as well as being able to work to strict deadlines.

Nail technician

You will need to be qualified to Level 2 or Level 3 standard and will specialize in carrying out treatments for the nail such as manicures, pedicures, artificial nail application, and nail art. Recognized qualifications include:

◎ NVQ/SVQ Levels 2 and 3 in Nail Services
◎ Vocational Training Charitable Trust (VTCT) Level 2 Certificate in Nail treatments.

Opportunities for nail technicians are growing. You could work on a mobile basis or in a salon with other technicians, beauticians, hairdressers, or therapists. There are jobs in nail bars in large department stores, airports, and shopping centres. Work is often available producing spectacular nails for photoshoots or fashion shows. Courses for nail technicians are offered by many colleges.

Jolene is a nail technician.

My first client arrives around 8.30 a.m., and I usually see around six to eight clients a day. The treatments can be quite varied, from a file and revarnish to a full set of gel overlays. I enjoy the more creative work such as diamanté and French nail art painting. I also give clients advice on how to look after their nails. The fumes from the products means that you need to have good ventilation in the salon, as well as taking regular breaks.

In between clients I find time to provide training for the junior nail technician. Today, I watched her do a full set of acrylic nails for her first assessment.

My day ends around 6.00 p.m., after I have cleared away my work station and filed the client records.

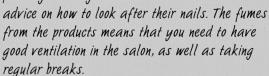

LEIGHTON DENNY

Leighton Denny has won Nail Technician of the Year award so many times, he's been banned from entering and made a judge instead! He has several salons, his own brand of nail products, and does photoshoots all around the world. His celebrity clients include Joan Collins, Kate Moss, and Davina McCall, and his nails have been hailed as the "ultimate accessory" in top glossy magazines. Leighton started out as a forklift truck driver. Following a trip to the United States he returned to Bradford, Yorkshire, to train as a nail technician. He then started up as a freelance nail technician, pampering guests on cruise liners around the world before opening his first boutique salon.

Sales representative

You will have a minimum of NVQ/SVQ Level 2 in Beauty or Hairdressing. You will visit businesses such as beauty salons, hairdressers, and health spas to try to sell your company's products. These can be skin or hair products, make-up, or equipment.

Product trainer

You will teach people how to use certain types of beauty products, to enable them to carry out treatments and sell them to clients. You will need to know everything about the products and you will spend lots of time on the road with overnight stays in hotels. You may be paid **commission**.

Beauty consultant/demonstrators

You may work in a department store selling and demonstrating skincare, make-up, and perfume products. You will do makeovers and lessons for customers, in the hope of selling products. Your appearance must be perfect at all times and you will usually wear a uniform provided by the cosmetic company that you work for. You will also set up displays of promotional material and keep stock records.

Get ahead!

These are some of the qualifications which will give you the advantage as a beauty consultant or demonstrator:
• Certificate in Cosmetic Make-up and Beauty Consultancy (sales): this covers basic beauty treatments, marketing cosmetics and perfumes, and stock control.
• Local colleges may run courses such as the Diploma in Cosmetic Make-Up or Beauty Consultant Diploma.

As a beauty consultant/ demonstrator, you can work all over the UK, as well as overseas, for example, in large hotels, airports, and on cruise ships. The right personality and attitude are more important than formal qualifications, but you will need to have a good level of literacy, numeracy, and organizational skills.

Health and fitness instructors

Health and fitness instructors usually work in gyms or leisure centres, teaching group exercise classes or giving one-to-one tuition. They may also give advice on **nutrition** and lifestyle. Instructors work long and unsociable hours, including some evenings and weekends. There is more flexibility if you are self-employed, but you will still need to work when your customers need you.

You will need good GCSE grades in Science, because a sound knowledge of **anatomy** and body systems is essential. You will also need to study for specialist qualifications such as:

◎ NVQ/SVQ Level 2 or 3 in Instructing Exercise and Fitness
◎ NVQ/SVQ in Sport, Recreation, and Allied Occupations.

Personal trainers

Personal trainers motivate, instruct, and guide clients in order to help them get or keep fit. They often design exercise plans for clients to follow when exercising alone. Most personal trainers are freelance and charge clients by the hour. Trainers' skills can include many fitness subjects, for example, aerobics, weight training, circuit training, keep fit, and yoga.

Qualifications for personal trainers

◎ Premier Training and Development Diploma: a full diploma in exercise, nutrition, and sports therapy
◎ CHEK Institute – Levels 1–4 CHEK practitioner
◎ Young Men's Christian Assocation (YMCA) – Diploma in Personal Training.

right: *A big part of a personal trainer's job is keeping the client motivated to work out.*

Massage therapist

Massage therapists carry out massage techniques on the soft body tissue and muscles of clients in order to relax, improve well-being, stimulate, or heal. There are many types of massage available, for example, Swedish, Sports, Physiotherapy, and **Lymphatic Drainage**, to name a few. You could work in a hair and beauty salon, beauty clinic, health farm, spa, sports club, or even a hospital.

To qualify as a masseur you will usually complete a 1- or 2-year full-time course to Level 3 standard, which will cover all the anatomy, **physiology**, and body systems you need to know.

Qualifications for masseurs

◎ Level 1 Certificate in Understanding Personal Therapies: this provides a simple introduction for those under 16 in school link programmes
◎ NVQ/SVQ Level 2 in Beauty Therapy
◎ NVQ/SVQ Level 3 in Beauty Therapy (massage route)
◎ ITEC in Anatomy, Physiology, and Body Massage.

CASE STUDY

Roy is a freelance masseur. He describes a typical working day below.

I get up at 7.00a.m. and check my day's appointments so I can plan my day. I travel to my first appointment at 8.30a.m., at the local health and sports club, where I complete two full body massages on club members after their workouts. When I have finished, I have a quick swim in the club.

At 11.30a.m. I travel to my next appointment at a local business. There I carry out head, neck, and shoulder massages to employees over the lunchtime period. I finish at 3.00p.m., when I have a late lunch.

After lunch, I see my next client – a sportswoman who needs some deep massage to help relieve pain from a muscle injury. My day ends at 4.30p.m.

Some days I work until 8 or 9.00p.m. at night because a lot of my clients need appointments to fit around their work. I have a 2-hour break in the day if I work evenings as the work is very tiring, and you cannot give a good treatment if you are tired yourself.

Holistic therapy

After training many massage therapists decide to train further to specialize in holistic therapies such as reflexology. As a holistic therapist you will be trained in complementary therapies, such as Indian head massage, aromatherapy, Reiki, reflexology, and **Thermo-auricular Therapy**, which are designed to improve the well-being and health of the client. You may specialize in one or more treatments, and work in a range of settings such as health clubs, medical clinics, hospitals, beauty salons, cruise ships, nursing homes, or clients' own homes. Most holistic therapists are self-employed.

right: *In reflexology, pressure is applied to areas of the feet that correspond to different parts of the body. There are around 15,000 reflexologists currently practising in the UK.*

Courses for holistic therapy range from a 2-year part-time diploma to a 3- or 4-year full-time degree. You will need a good GCSE grade in Biology. Recognized qualifications include:

- ◉ NVQ/SVQ Level 3 in Beauty Therapy (holistic route)
- ◉ VTCT and ITEC also have a range of holistic courses.

Opportunities in the UK and beyond!

The jobs covered in this chapter can take you to many different places of work around the UK and abroad! The spider diagram below gives you some idea of the vast range of places you might end up working in.

Get ahead!

Choose from the list below and find out as much as you can about that aspect of holistic therapy:
- Reiki
- Hot stone massage
- Reflexology
- Aromatherapy
- Crystal healing
- Thermal auricular therapy
- Indian head massage.

What can you find out about the hours, training, qualifications, and working conditions involved? What can you expect to be paid?

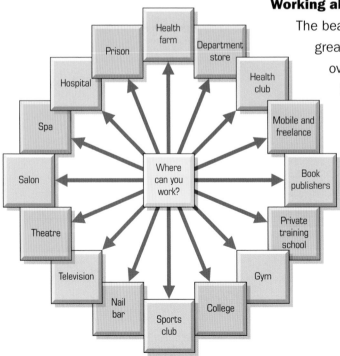

Working abroad

The beauty industry also offers great opportunities to work overseas. You could work in all the locations covered in the spider diagram, in a range of different countries. If you are very lucky, you could also work abroad on:

- ◉ cruise ships
- ◉ film sets
- ◉ airlines
- ◉ magazine and catalogue shoots.

Think fantastic jobs like these don't exist? Well think again! Many of the industry magazines are full of opportunities for the right people.

CASE STUDY

Mai is an airline beauty therapist.

My working day starts when I board the flight and go through to the beauty therapy area of upper class where we organize the treatment area. If we're not already fully booked, I may speak to the passengers as they take their seats and ask if anyone wishes to have a treatment during their flight. Typical treatments that we offer are:

- *massages to calm and get rid of headaches*
- *hand treatments to get rid of dead dry skin, massage, and moisturize*
- *mini manicures which include filing, buffing, and* **cuticle** *work*
- *head, neck, or shoulder massages.*

The work is enjoyable, but very tiring as you are on your feet all day and need to look your best at all times.

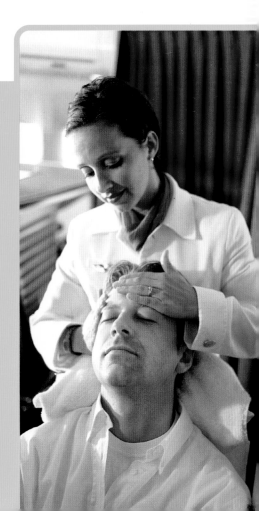

Chapter 2

Treatments of the trade

So, you would like to follow a career in the beauty industry. But do you know what this will involve? Working in beauty is not just a case of applying make-up, shampooing hair, or waxing a person's legs! If you think you want to be part of this industry, make sure you know what you will be expected to do. This chapter will help you to understand something of what is involved in the day-to-day business of the beauty industry.

Basic treatments and activities

Beauty treatments

◎ *Aromatherapy*: **essential oils** extracted from plants and herbs are used to improve a wide variety of conditions, relieve stress, and induce relaxation. The essential oils can be used in massage oils, rubs, inhalations, and baths.

◎ *Electrical face and body treatments*: a range of electrical equipment is used to achieve better muscle and skin tone. Some treatments aid slimming and improve the appearance of cellulite on the body.

◎ *Electrical epilation/electrolysis*: the removal of unwanted hair through the application of a low-level electrical current from a **probe** inserted into the hair **follicle**. This will damage the root structure; eventually the treatment can permanently destroy the hair.

◎ *Eye treatments*: this can be lash and brow tinting which is used to darken the natural lashes; eyebrow shaping to enhance the natural shape of the brow; or eyelash perming to curl the lashes. False lashes can be applied to increase the length and thickness of the lashes.

◎ *Heat and bath treatments*: hydrotherapy (water therapy) can be very effective in relieving stress, aches, and pains and as a pre-heating treatment prior to massage.

- *Indian head massage*: also know as Champissage, this is an ancient technique that involves massaging and rubbing the head, neck, and shoulders. It is used for stress relief and improved circulation to the scalp.
- *Make-up*: products used to enhance the natural appearance of the skin and facial features. Make-up effects can be for day, evening, corrective, dramatic, theatrical, photographic, or media.

above: *Nail artists can get really creative with patterns and glitter!*

- *Manicures and pedicures*: involves treatment on the skin of the hands and feet, the nails, and the surrounding cuticles. Products are used to massage, remove dead dry skin, soften, shape, and polish.
- *Manual body massage*: usually Swedish massage, it involves movements by the hands across the body which are used to improve blood flow, exercise the muscles, and relax the body.
- *Manual facial*: a treatment to deep cleanse the skin, which can also include a massage of the face, neck, and shoulders. No electrical equipment is used – it is all hands-on.
- *Nail techniques*: this involves applying extensions to the natural nail with gel or acrylic. Nail techniques also include nail art.
- *Reflexology*: consists of pressure massage on the reflex points of the hands or feet. These reflex points mirror other parts of the body. The treatment unblocks the energy lines to aid self-healing and body re-balancing.

- *Spray tan*: a temporary tanning lotion or spray is applied to the body using a spray machine or air brush, to deepen the natural skin tone.
- *Ultra violet (UV) tanning*: tanning of the skin by application of ultra-violet rays from a sunbed or solarium. This must be closely monitored by experienced staff to avoid permanent damage to the skin.
- *Wax depilation*: the removal of unwanted hair on the body, usually from the legs, underarm, bikini, and facial area. Warm wax is applied to the skin and sticks to the hairs. When paper or fabric strips are applied to the wax and then pulled off, the hairs are removed from the root.

above: *Waxing is a real hands-on job, so you must be comfortable touching other people's bodies to carry out this treatment.*

Hair

- *Cutting*: from trimming the hair to complete re-styling, cutting involves specialized methods of cutting, shaving, and thinning.
- *Perming and relaxing*: curlers are put through the hair and chemicals are then applied to the hair to change its structure. The hair then keeps the curls after the curlers are removed. The same chemicals can also be used for relaxing and straightening hair.
- *Colouring*: colour can be applied to the hair as a whole block colour or in sections using different techniques and colouring chemicals.
- *Setting*: hair is put in curlers and dried thoroughly under the drier, sometimes with the use of setting products and lotions.

- *Blow drying*: sleek, smooth hair or curls and flicks can be achieved by using a hair dryer and different brushes.
- *Straightening*: straightening irons are used, usually on dry hair. The hot irons are run through the hair to smooth the cuticle so that the hair is straight and glossy.
- *Wigmaking*: wigs and hairpieces can be created by weaving natural or synthetic hair.

Make-up

- *Day and evening make-up*: a variety of techniques and products are applied to improve and enhance a person's natural features.
- *Cosmetic camouflage*: waterproof, dense make-up is applied with various brushes and sponges. It is used to cover up scars, birthmarks, burns, and blemishes.
- *Theatrical*: make-up is applied to change a person's appearance completely, to alter his or her look for a different time in history, or to match costumes.
- *Television and media*: make-up is applied that withstands the hot, bright glare of the studio lights and makes the presenters features stand out on camera. Applying make-up for film and television productions involves using techniques that help create a person's character, for example, adding false noses, beards, and cuts and scars.
- *Fantasy and face painting*: characters or designs can be painted onto the body and face. Children's face painting is popular and simple to do, but more advanced painting skills can create spectacular illusions.

right: *Face painting like this requires great skill and creativity, and the results can look amazing.*

Fitness

◎ *Aerobics*: high impact, strenuous exercise sessions to music, usually performed in a group with an instructor showing you what to do. Good fun, but hard work!

◎ *Running/jogging*: it is far easier to run or jog with a personal trainer driving you forwards – you have fewer excuses to stop!

◎ *Pilates*: uses muscle strengthening techniques to improve fitness and posture. The movements are small and very controlled, so this exercise is good for all ages.

◎ *Yoga*: strengthens and lengthens the muscles, improves posture and balance, and helps breathing. Many believe yoga relaxes and improves the mind as well as the body.

◎ *Weight training*: the use of fixed or free weights. Muscles are strengthened and toned over time.

Get ahead!

Find out about another treatment or method that is not covered here. Carry out your own research at local beauty salons, hairdressers, and health centres. You could also do some research on the Internet and in the library.

left: *Yoga and Pilates are very popular, and there is a high demand for instructors.*

CASE STUDY

Jamie Lloyd is a personal trainer. Visit his website at www.jlpersonaltraining.com.

I am a freelance personal trainer part-time and also work as a full-time firefighter with the London Fire Brigade. I have always been actively involved in fitness since the age of 6, but it all started when I did a degree in Sports Science at the Roehampton Institute, London. I then worked as a personal trainer and gym instructor at two health clubs in London.

I have a range of clients and they come in all shapes, sizes, and abilities. I have trained a former professional tennis player, a **Coronation Street** actress, and a veteran triathlete from the Great Britain squad. I also train people recovering from illnesses and pregnancies. This is what makes my job interesting, as I get to meet and work with people from all walks of life.

To be successful you have to be patient and organized, as there is a lot of time spent calling clients, making and changing appointments, and planning routines. You also have to find time to keep up your own fitness. Lots of work is done in the early morning and in the evenings, but I love it, especially when I see clients progress and achieve their goals.

The earnings for a personal trainer vary. You can earn around £15 an hour if you are working in a health club, but if you are your own boss and are good at what you do, then you can expect to earn £45 an hour.

I am always studying and researching articles to continue my education. I spend around £3,000 a year on courses to keep up my membership status on the National Register of Personal Trainers and on the Exercise Register. This means I can stay ahead of the rest and provide the best possible service to my clients!

right: Personal trainers meet with their clients to discuss their fitness needs.

Chapter 3

Tools of the trade

In the beauty industry, the special qualities that you have to offer your employers and your clients are more important than academic skills. People skills are especially important – the ability to **interact** with all types of people, regardless of age, ethnicity, gender, or personality, is essential.

Another key skill in the beauty industry is the ability to make clients feel at ease. You will do this by demonstrating good conversational skills. Awkward silences and unnatural conversations just make people feel embarrassed and self-conscious, especially when the type of treatment or activity being carried out is of a very personal nature. It is also no good being squeamish about touching people and parts of their body, or being embarrassed to tell people what to do.

Important qualities for working in the beauty industry

◎ Good communication skills – you must be good at explaining how products, treatments, and activities work.
◎ Smart appearance and awareness of the importance of good hygiene.
◎ A friendly and welcoming manner that puts clients at ease.
◎ Patience and good listening skills.
◎ A positive attitude – showing confidence and belief in the job you do.
◎ A caring and respectful manner.
◎ **Stamina** and strength – you will be on your feet all day and sometimes the work can be strenuous.
◎ Good health and a high level of fitness.

NOT FOR YOU…

Unfortunately, there are some things which may mean a career in the beauty industry is not for you:
◎ a history of backache and back problems
◎ allergies to cosmetic and hair products.

- An artistic flair, for example, for nail art and make-up.
- Some knowledge of anatomy, physiology, and chemistry.
- The ability to sell products and promote treatments and services to clients.
- Good teamwork skills and the ability to get on with a wide range of colleagues.

A healthy you

To be a success in the beauty industry you need to understand the importance and benefits of a healthy lifestyle – health and beauty are strong partners!

In order to stay in top condition the body needs:

- a good balanced diet and regular meals, with healthy low-fat snacks in between
- regular fresh air and exercise
- lots of water to flush out toxins
- plenty of sleep to rest and repair.

Get ahead!

The beauty industry is a caring profession, so make sure you are definitely a "people person" before you start to consider a career in beauty. Think about how you interact with your friends, your family, and with strangers. Ask people you trust to give you a truthful assessment of how well they think you would do in this type of industry.

BE HEALTHY!

Healthy lifestyles for you and your clients lead to:
- hair that glistens and shines
- skin that is smooth and clear
- brightness and enthusiasm for the day ahead
- energy and staying power.

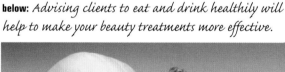
below: *Advising clients to eat and drink healthily will help to make your beauty treatments more effective.*

There are other factors to consider for a healthy lifestyle.

◎ Too much sunbathing can dry out the skin and hair and cause the skin to age early.

◎ Smoking can cause the skin to become sensitive, red, and blotchy. Tobacco and nicotine in cigarettes also uses up important vitamins and minerals that the body needs to work well. Smoking makes teeth turn yellow and clothes and skin smell. All in all, not good for a career in beauty!

CASE STUDY

Jez tells us about qualities needed to be in the industry.

I am a qualified hair and beauty therapist, yes – even men do beauty therapy! Don't even think about it, though, unless you really believe it's for you. It's hard work standing on your feet all day. You need a lot of patience, and must be a good listener – everyone tells you their problems. Of course, this also means that you are trusted with private information and you musn't break people's confidentiality.

Also you need to get on with all the different people you will work with. You need to be fair to all, and able to work in a team. Remember, you can't be friends with everyone, but you must be able to get on with them.

Get ahead!

In the beauty industry, clients will look up to you for your skills and expertise. You will also be asked for advice and guidance, so it is important that you practise what you recommend.

left: *You should try to keep your look modern, neat, and clean.*

Chapter 4

What's the story?

In this chapter you will find out about what it is really like to work in the beauty industry by looking at case studies from real people. Their accounts will give you a taste of what your day will be like and the pay and **perks** you can expect.

Beauty salon assistant

Jemma is 15 and is completing her **National Vocational Qualification** (NVQ) Level 1 Beauty Therapy at school, 1 day a week. The rest of the week she has a normal school timetable.

Training

"My school timetable means that I complete my NVQ Level 1 qualification as part of a work-related learning programme. This consists of supported study, key skills training, and industry visits, 1 day per week training as a beauty therapist, and the rest of the week carrying out school subjects such as Maths, English, and Science. It's a real mixture and means that I don't get bored as there is always a lot going on."

above: *Your clients will feel more at ease if you dress smartly and look **professional**.*

Responsibilities

"As part of my beauty training I sometimes have to assist the Level 2 students by helping them set up their trolleys and work area, and by helping them with clients."

The highs

"Carrying out treatments on each other for manicures and facials and learning about how cool a career in beauty can be. I'd really like to travel with my job."

The lows

"I have quite a lot of written work, as I have to complete a **portfolio** to show evidence, but my tutor is a real help and I can go to her if I get stuck."

Special qualities

"You must be patient and have a caring personality when you are dealing with clients and must not bring your problems to work. It's a bit like being like an actress – even though you might be having a bad day you must not let your clients know."

"I read lots of glossy magazines and love the model's make-up, reading about new beauty products, and seeing all the different nail colours and nail art. This was why I began to think that I'd like to try beauty as a career."

Tools of the trade

"You have to have a manicure kit plus some facial materials like headbands. But there isn't too much that you need for Level 1 as the products are supplied by the school."

In the future

"I would like to do NVQ Level 2 (make-up route) as I want to specialize in the make-up side of the business. Hopefully, I will get a job as an assistant to a make-up artist."

Hardships?

"There are none! Not in my opinion, anyway, but maybe there will be when I get a job. At the moment I am happy being at school and being able to study what I want instead of just doing Maths, English, and Science."

Trainee hairdresser

Jamal left school to train as a hairdresser at his local college. He is working towards an NVQ Level 1 in Hairdressing 4 days a week, with 1 day's work experience in a salon. He helps in the salon, carrying out a wide range of jobs, from shampooing, sweeping the floor, passing up curlers and foil, to making tea for clients.

above: *Hair salons must be kept very neat and tidy, and it is usually a trainee hairdresser who will sweep up after haircuts.*

Training

"My timetable has a mixture of theory and practical lessons. The theory is important, because you need to learn about health and safety and science, as well as just being able to do people's hair. We have real clients who visit us at college so that we can practise on them to build evidence for our portfolio. We also do Key Skills and go to a local hairdressing salon to get more experience in a real setting. Our tutor visits us and assesses us on-the-job."

Your responsibilities

"I help with shampooing and drying customers' hair, reception duties, answering the telephone, making appointments, sorting towels and gowns, and helping clients with their coats and bags. I also sweep up, clean up, and make drinks! Basically I am there to be a help to the stylists."

The highs

"Everyone is friendly, the salon is very up-market and trendy, and I love the practical side of the work."

The lows

"An achy back and legs from standing all day!"

Special qualities

"You must be happy, friendly, not ever grumpy, and able to move quickly between jobs because time is short. You also need to be able to look around constantly to see what needs doing and what might need doing soon, as well as keeping ahead of the next client that is due in. You also have to be creative and good with people. You need to be able to handle money properly, use a till, and meet and greet people."

Why hairdressing?

"I always loved doing my friend's hair. I had a careers meeting at school and was given more information about how to train. I made my mind up then and there that this is what I was going to do."

Tools of the trade

"Apart from the hairdryers in the salon, everyone has their own hairdressing kit, which they have to supply. It contains combs, brushes, and scissors."

In the future

"I would like to do Level 2 so I can learn cutting and blow drying – and maybe even Level 3, but I'm not too sure yet. After that I would like to get some experience before hopefully opening my own salon in the future."

Hardships?

"I am **dyslexic** and, when I started, I was panicking that I would have to use the till and write down client appointments. But my boss was very understanding and introduced me slowly until I felt confident that I could do it."

Pay and perks

What will your annual income be?

These figures are only a guide, as actual rates of pay may vary depending on the employer and where people live.

Beauty therapist

◎ Newly qualified therapists earn about £10,000 per year.

◎ Experienced therapists could earn between £10,000 and £15,000 a year.

◎ A salon manager or owner could earn between £15,000 and £30,000 a year.

◎ A self-employed therapist specializing in a particular field could earn up to £40,000 or more.

Clients' tips and commission for products sold after a treatment can boost income. Bonus schemes are also common in larger centres.

The **National Minimum Wage** (NMW) became law from 1 April 1999, and therefore it is an offence for an employer to pay an employee less than this. From 1 October 2006 the NMW entitles:

◎ staff over 22 to earn at least £5.35 per hour

◎ staff aged 18–21 who are training at least £4.45 per hour while they are working

◎ young workers aged 16–17 at least £3.30 per hour.

If you are on an apprenticeship you will not be entitled to the minimum wage until the age of 19. Alternatively, if you are over the age of 26 and on an apprenticeship you will not be entitled to the NMW until you have worked for 12 months as an apprentice.

left: *The financial rewards in the beauty industry range from fairly low to quite high.*

Store demonstrator

◎ Starting salary for a full-time store demonstrator is around £10,000.
◎ More experienced store demonstrators can expect to earn between £12,250 and £16,000.
◎ Agency-employed demonstrators can earn between £50 and £60 for a day's work. They may be paid commission, based on the number of sales made during a promotion.

Beauty consultants

◎ Start on around £8,500 a year.
◎ Experienced consultants can earn £13,000.
◎ Area managers can earn up to £30,000.

Hairdressing

◎ Salaries range from between £8,000 and £30,000.

Nail technician

◎ A newly qualified nail technician will probably earn around £10,000 a year.
◎ This could rise to between £10,000 and £12,000.
◎ Self-employed nail technicians can earn much more than this.

Massage therapist

◎ The starting salary for a masseur/masseuse is around £10,000 a year.
◎ More experienced practitioners working in a salon earn between £15,000 and £19,000.
◎ Many practitioners are self-employed and will charge a session or hourly rate, ranging from between £15 and £60.

Reflexologist

Most reflexologists are self-employed, so income varies according to the number of patients they treat and the amount they charge for each session.

◎ Someone building a practice could earn £12,000 a year.
◎ With experience this could increase to £20,000.
◎ Reflexologists with large, established practices could earn £40,000.

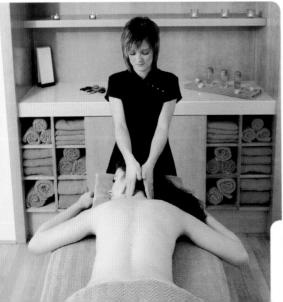

left: *Masseurs need to ensure their treatment room is perfectly clean and tidy.*

Aromatherapist
◎ Earnings start at around £12,000 a year.
◎ Self-employed aromatherapists can charge by the hour or per treatment – approximately £30 per hour.

Coaches/fitness instructors
◎ Earnings start at around £11,000 rising to about £30,000 for experienced instructors.

Personal trainers
◎ As most personal trainers are self-employed they usually charge clients on an hourly basis. The average rate is £40 per hour. They may also work part-time, combining this with another job.

Make-up artists
Most make-up artists work freelance and are paid fees per contract/project. The following figures are possible annual equivalents:
◎ New make-up artists earn from around £15,000 a year.
◎ Make-up artists with experience can earn between £16,000 and £25,000.

Get ahead!

These figures are only a guideline and much higher salaries are now being earned in an industry that was once very poorly paid. Jobs such as product trainers and spa managers can demand excellent wages in line with their experience and expertise.

What are the perks of the job?

A job in the beauty industry has always provided a bonus – the chance to be pampered yourself. This is especially important as you need to look as well-groomed and relaxed as your clients. If there is a gap in the appointments column and all other jobs are done, then it is accepted that staff can carry out treatments or practise new skills on each other, as long as it doesn't affect their work.

Incentives on offer in some companies include commission payments based on your sales and occasionally your treatments – particularly if you are a productive member of staff who brings in a good profit for them. Commission can typically be 10 per cent of your takings, so this can certainly boost your weekly wage.

Still unsure about which area of the beauty industry you would like to work in? Try this quiz to help you!

1 Do you like set routines?
a) Always
b) Never
c) Sometimes

2 What do you prefer?
a) The natural look
b) The glamorous look
c) The healthy look

3 Do you like to work in a large group?
a) Quite often
b) Most of the time
c) Occasionally

4 Why do you want to work in the beauty industry?
a) To make people feel good
b) To make people look good
c) To boost people's fitness and knowledge

5 Do you like to travel?
a) Never
b) A lot
c) A little

6 Do you like to make all your own decisions?
a) Sometimes
b) Most of the time
c) Always

If you scored...

◎ *Mostly a)*: you are most suited to a job in a high street salon as you like to know exactly how your day will be and don't like the unexpected. You need to be in control, be able to plan, and have the security of a regular job.

◎ *Mostly b)*: you like the unexpected and excitement, so you are suited to jobs that involve travel, new experiences, and change such as working on photoshoots, on cruise liners, or as an airline therapist.

◎ *Mostly c)*: you enjoy trying new things and learning different techniques, and sometimes you like to broaden your horizons, but only as long as you have control and know exactly what is expected of you. Jobs such as personal training, mobile therapy, and freelance hairdressing will suit you best, as will working as a sales representative, trainer, or teacher.

Chapter 5

The first step

Your life at school may at times seem uninspiring because you don't seem to understand how Maths or Science can help you in your career . . . but read on. All the skills and knowledge you pick up at school will help you in some way, whether this contribution is large or small, at some point in your life.

How your studies at school can help

Science

◎ Biology lessons will provide you with essential knowledge about anatomy and physiology.

◎ Chemistry will help you to understand how products are made. If you are interested in cosmetics and skincare, it is always good to know about the ingredients.

◎ In your Physics lessons you will learn about electricity and temperature. These are important because you may operate electrical and heat machines for slimming, skincare, hair care, and fitness.

Maths (including Key Skills in numeracy)

No business will be successful if the staff are not able to take correct payment for treatments and give the correct change. Even with the use of a calculator or till it is still essential that you are able to understand simple calculations!

right: *There is a lot of science behind the products that you will use as part of your treatments in the beauty industry.*

Get ahead!

Try to work out the costs for the following:

Your salon charges £15.00 for a full-leg wax which takes 45 minutes.

- The therapist is paid £6.00 per hour.
- The products cost 50p for the treatment.
- The heat and light costs £1.00 per hour.
- The rent costs £2.00 per hour.

How much profit does the salon make?

Information technology (Key Skills)

Salons, health clubs, and hairdressers need thorough client information records and all this data is usually stored on a computer. You will also operate electronic tills and perhaps also electronic appointment booking systems. A knowledge of word processing is useful as you may need to design posters and mail shots and brochures to advertise your business or treatment.

English

English lessons are essential because they teach you about grammar and spelling. These are important for writing down appointments, completing client records, and completing application forms and **curriculum vitae** (CVs).

Communication (Key Skills)

It is essential that you are able to demonstrate clear and positive methods of communication at all times. If both your spoken communication and your body language is positive, you will put clients at ease and give them confidence in you.

Art

Beauty is a very creative career. You do not necessarily need to be able to paint pictures, but you will need to be able to plan and think of imaginative ideas, especially if you want a career in make-up or hair.

left: *Basic computing skills are a requirement for most jobs in the beauty industry.*

above: *You will build confidence in speaking and moving around in your Drama lessons.*

Drama

Drama lessons will teach you how to carry yourself and your voice well. They also give you confidence in speaking clearly to a large group of people.

How your everyday life experiences can help

People skills

An open face and friendly nature make people easier to approach and work with. Try to develop these! Practise chatting to people you do not know. Think of subjects that you could talk about that will be interesting to just about everyone. Smile a lot and maintain eye contact, and you will get on much better with all sorts of people.

Telephone skills

These are important for making appointments, giving information, and ordering products and equipment. The way that you chat to your friends on the telephone is not the way that you should talk when you are at work. Slang words such as *hiya*, *yeah*, and *dunno* are not acceptable. If you get into the habit now of speaking properly on the telephone it will help you in the future.

Get ahead!

Write a list of all the greetings and words that you think should not be used on the telephone. Then write another list, of all the words that should be used.

Time management and organizational skills

You must be organized in the beauty industry. You need to set up for your treatments, make sure you finish in time for the next client, and not keep clients waiting. If you are hopeless at getting up in the morning, for example, make sure that you have all your clothes ready the night before and your bag, uniform, and equipment packed.

Get ahead!

Write out a week's timetable with details of your social life, eating, sleeping, chilling out time, and study time (make sure you have enough study time!). Try and keep to this timetable for a week to see if it improves your time management.

Teamworking

You will work with a wide range of people in the beauty industry and meet all sorts of different characters. Everyone has slightly different ways of working! It is important that you understand how a good team works together, supporting each other, to make a successful business. Part of teamworking is learning to put differences aside and moving forward to solve any problems. The next time your friends have a disagreement, don't side with one of them or get involved. Instead, try to see both sides of the argument and make some positive suggestions about solving it.

above: *Working in small groups or teams can help you to develop good teamworking skills.*

Chapter 6

A foot in the door

So, you now have an idea about what you might like to do when you leave school. However, most of the time the reality of work is not quite how you imagine it! Work experience and work-related learning will help by giving you a glimpse of the realities of working in your industry. By trying out a job during work experience you may find that that it is even better than you thought . . . or you may realize that actually it is not for you.

Work-related learning in Years 10 and 11

Your school will help you by planning work-related activities that help you to make decisions about your career and prepare you for getting a job when you leave school. For some of you, this will take the place of an extended work-related learning programme with a Further Education (FE) college, training provider, employer, or in Year 11. This may include working towards National Vocational Qualifications (NVQs) or Scottish Vocational Qualifications (SVQs).

Activities will be planned that will help you.

◎ *Learn through work*: experiences of work such as work and community visits, **placements**, work experience, and part-time jobs.
◎ *Learn about work*: opportunities provided by vocational courses and careers education that cover topics such as running a business, setting up a business, money and finance, and employees' rights.
◎ *Prepare for work*: developing personal qualities and attitudes needed for a job, identifying key skills, and planning for lifelong learning. Industry visits, mock interviews, and role-play activities may be carried out.

Work experience

Work experience is often your first taste of working for a real employer in a real company. It can help you prepare for working life by helping you understand the importance of the need for discipline at work, punctuality, employment contracts, health and safety, **risk assessments** and how to deal with **hazards**, and the hours of work required of employees in different jobs.

In a short placement, work experience is usually carried out for a short block during the school year, typically 2 weeks in the summer term. Extended placements are longer than the standard 1- or 2-week block. Lots of choices for extended placements are available and it can take the form of 1 or 2 days each week over a period of 1 or 2 years.

Getting the placement

You may be asked to write a letter of introduction to your placement employer.

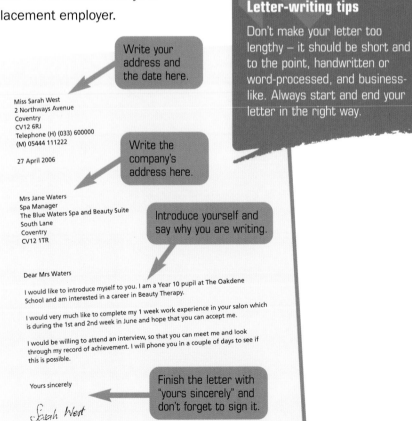

Write your address and the date here.

Write the company's address here.

Introduce yourself and say why you are writing.

Finish the letter with "yours sincerely" and don't forget to sign it.

Get ahead!

Letter-writing tips

Don't make your letter too lengthy – it should be short and to the point, handwritten or word-processed, and business-like. Always start and end your letter in the right way.

Miss Sarah West
2 Northways Avenue
Coventry
CV12 6RJ
Telephone (H) (033) 600000
(M) 05444 111222

27 April 2006

Mrs Jane Waters
Spa Manager
The Blue Waters Spa and Beauty Suite
South Lane
Coventry
CV12 1TR

Dear Mrs Waters

I would like to introduce myself to you. I am a Year 10 pupil at The Oakdene School and am interested in a career in Beauty Therapy.

I would very much like to complete my 1 week work experience in your salon which is during the 1st and 2nd week in June and hope that you can accept me.

I would be willing to attend an interview, so that you can meet me and look through my record of achievement. I will phone you in a couple of days to see if this is possible.

Yours sincerely

Sarah West

Sarah West

Preparing for an interview

Before you are selected by the employer as a work experience student, you may have to attend an interview for your work placement. To best prepare for this, find out a bit about the company and the job that you are going for. You can then plan some questions to ask the interviewer about the job – after all, the interview is also an opportunity for you to find out about that particular job and company. Some questions you might want to ask are:

Get ahead!

Partner up and plan an interview. One of you is the interviewee and the other the interviewer. Think up some questions and answers and then carry out a role-play exercise to practise your interview skills.

- ◎ Who will I report to?
- ◎ What are my hours and responsibilities?
- ◎ Do you offer staff training?
- ◎ When will I know whether I have been selected?

To give you the best chance in the interview, be sure to practise some typical interview questions and answers. A few examples are listed below – remember, there are many more that you may ask or be asked!

INTERVIEW Q&A

- ◎ What qualities can you bring to our company?
- ◎ Why do you want to work for this company?
- ◎ What do you think that this job involves?
- ◎ What are your strengths and weaknesses?
- ◎ How would your friends and family describe you?
- ◎ Give an example of when you have worked well in a team.
- ◎ What do you think you would dislike about this job?
- ◎ How do you organize your time?
- ◎ What did you learn from your work experience?

The day of the interview

You should dress to impress: wear smart, clean clothes and shoes; your hair should be neat and clean; your nails well manicured and fairly short. If you wear make-up, apply only modest amounts.

Get ahead!

Being late for an interview will give a very bad impression. To avoid this, practise and time the journey there before the day of your interview. Then, on the day of the interview, allow some extra journey time to ensure that you will not be late.

You should take with you to each interview:

◎ the invitation to interview letter
◎ a record of achievement (if you are a school leaver or student)
◎ certificates or diplomas
◎ your small equipment/tools, such as tweezers and brushes, if you are doing trade tests
◎ a small list of questions about the job.

During the interview, remember to:

◎ smile and be friendly
◎ be yourself
◎ maintain good posture when walking in to the room and sitting down
◎ use positive body language with good eye contact.

WHAT COULD COST YOU THE JOB?

◎ Being late or unprepared for the interview
◎ Sloppy appearance, for example, unironed clothes, chipped nails, greasy hair
◎ Being negative about your skills and making excuses
◎ Limp handshake and lack of eye contact
◎ Being unable to answer many of the questions asked
◎ Speaking lazily, for example, dropped letters at the start and end of words along with the use of slang
◎ Too much make-up and jewellery
◎ Chewing gum
◎ Criticising someone (especially your teacher!)

Evidence for your work experience

After your work experience placement is over you will be expected to show evidence of what you have learned. This could be a portfolio, book, or folder, for example, which reflects all the different areas of work you took on.

Structuring your evidence portfolio

◎ Include a contents page at the beginning with chapter titles and page numbers or colour coding.

◎ Next, introduce your work experience. Write a short paragraph about where you went, what you did, and your reasons for going.

◎ Then write the main section. Be careful not to write too much – only what is necessary.

Write a little about each of the tasks that you had to undertake during your work experience. List any useful sources of information that have helped you. You could use bullet points and key points to give information to the reader, and use colour and underline for headings. Add pictures, photographs, leaflets, and diagrams for interest, and include real items if possible such as nail tips, hair pins, or brochures.

◎ Finally, add a conclusion at the end of your folder. State how you think that you have benefited from your work experience, for example, what you enjoyed doing most and what you found difficult.

Get ahead!

You can make your book or folder look really professional. You could decorate the front with your own artwork, for example, magazine cuttings or computer print-outs from relevant websites. Make sure that your folder or book is well organized. Use clear colour coding or page numbers throughout.

below: *You can create a thorough and well put-together record of your work experience.*

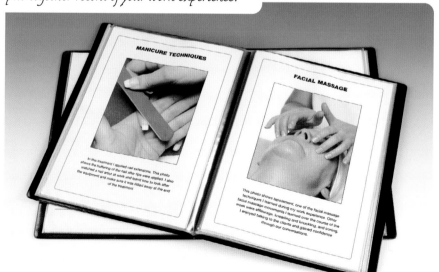

Giving a presentation

You may be expected to give a presentation of your work experience to your classmates. This will help to highlight what you have learnt and also gives information to others who may be thinking of a similar career. The presentation will also boost your skills and confidence in speaking and listening.

Tips for preparing a presentation

Your presentation should flow well from start to finish. Here are some tips for how to achieve this:

- Have an introduction to the job – what it was, where it was.
- Talk about the duties you were expected to carry out.
- Include what you learned and how it helped you.
- Keep it simple – stick to what you know or did.
- If possible, tell a funny story about something that may have happened to you at work.
- Conclude your presentation by saying whether you think it is the career for you. Explain why.

You could plan your talk by doing a mind map. You can add to each section as you think of things to say. When you have finished, you will have a well-organized plan.

below: *Giving a presentation will be informative for others and help to develop your communication skills.*

Once you have written your presentation, record yourself at home and play it back to yourself to check and time it. Or you could practise in front of your family or friends, then ask for their feedback.

Get ahead!

When giving the presentation, remember to speak clearly and make eye contact with your audience.

Chapter 7

A foot on the ladder

There is a wide range of courses and qualifications for working in the beauty industry in the UK. Which you decide to do depends on which type of training is best for you. If you don't like exams but prefer to be assessed regularly on your work, then a National Vocational Qualification (NVQ) might be your best choice. If you prefer to sit final examinations, then there are courses that offer this. Whatever qualification you choose to do, you can guarantee that it will help you to progress in your chosen career.

Vocational qualifications

Vocational qualifications mirror the skills and knowledge needed to do a job well. They allow you to gain the up-to-date skills that employers look for.

NVQs and SVQs

National Vocational Qualifications (NVQs) and Scottish Vocational Qualifications (SVQs) train you to actually do the job, not just talk about it. There are four levels:

◎ Level 1: usually a 1-year course that can be done 1–2 days a week whilst at school or at college.
◎ Level 2: usually a 1-year course that is studied on a full-time basis for 16–19 year olds. It is roughly equivalent to an A-level or a Higher.
◎ Level 3: usually a 1-year course which is taken after completing Level 2.
◎ Level 4: usually studied whilst at work on a part-time basis in order to learn about business and management sections of the beauty industry.

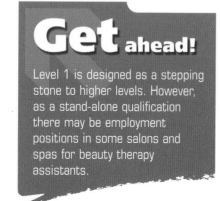

Get ahead!

Level 1 is designed as a stepping stone to higher levels. However, as a stand-alone qualification there may be employment positions in some salons and spas for beauty therapy assistants.

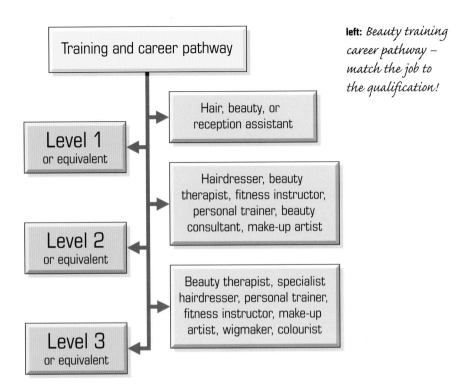

| Training and career pathway |

Level 1
or equivalent

Hair, beauty, or
reception assistant

Level 2
or equivalent

Hairdresser, beauty
therapist, fitness instructor,
personal trainer, beauty
consultant, make-up artist

Level 3
or equivalent

Beauty therapist, specialist
hairdresser, personal trainer,
fitness instructor, make-up
artist, wigmaker, colourist

left: *Beauty training career pathway – match the job to the qualification!*

Each NVQ/SVQ is made up of a number of units. These units are like building blocks that can be added together to make a complete qualification. Each unit is further divided into elements which describe in detail the skills and knowledge that a student needs. Each element has a set of **performance criteria** that you need to carry out to complete the unit successfully. These are strict requirements which must be met at every unit and every level in order for you to be judged **competent** at a particular skill.

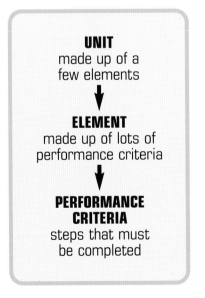

UNIT
made up of a
few elements

↓

ELEMENT
made up of lots of
performance criteria

↓

PERFORMANCE CRITERIA
steps that must
be completed

Where and how to train after school

Wherever you end up working, you cannot replace high-quality training on your path to success. Below are a few different ways to achieve this training.

Stay on at Years 12 and 13

If you are lucky enough to have a school that offers the vocational qualifications that you want to do, then staying on is a good option. You will be in an environment that is familiar to you, with people and teachers that know you and how you learn best.

Private training centre

The courses offered at private training centres are usually shorter and more **intensive**, with smaller class sizes. Not all private centres offer nationally recognized qualifications (qualifications that are accepted by employers and standard-setting bodies), so you must check what qualification you will get at the end.

Further Education (FE) college

At a college of further education the average length of training on a full-time course is 1 year for Level 2 and 2 years for Level 3. This can depend on:

◎ the GCSE grades that you achieved
◎ your previous work and other experiences
◎ your abilities
◎ your commitment and attitude.

Apprenticeships in hair and beauty

Apprentices learn on the job, building up knowledge and skills, gaining qualifications, and earning money at the same time. Apprenticeship schemes are aimed at training and developing skills for 16–24 year olds. The training is work-based, so provides excellent opportunity for work experience, as well as study. As a trainee you usually attend college 1 day a week and work in paid employment for the rest of the week.

Climbing the career ladder!

Although there are some excellent basic qualification courses available, you will not learn everything at college. Many skills can only be learned through experience and years in practice. This is especially true in the beauty industry. New techniques, products, and equipment mean that it is necessary to constantly update your skills and knowledge in order to keep standards high. You can continue to learn by taking short courses, which will widen your knowledge of what you have learned already.

Get ahead!

Map out a 5-year learning plan to expand your talents and flair and get a head start. For example:
- Year 1: I would like to get four GCSEs grade C
- Year 2: I would like to study for NVQ Level 2 in Hairdressing, and so on.

below: *You can go on a course to learn about new techniques such as hot stone massage.*

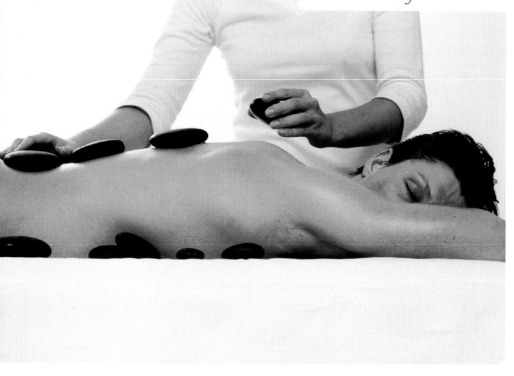

Gaining further experience

It is very important that you keep up to date with current trends and fashions so that you do not get left behind. You will need to spend time developing your knowledge and practising your skills. Attend trade shows, exhibitions, and workshops, and read trade magazines to find out about techniques, new products, cosmetic trends, trade events, and personalities influencing the trade.

Exhibitions are great places to see the new trends and products first-hand. The atmosphere is brilliant and the venues buzz with enthusiastic like-minded people from business owners to first-year college trainees.

Get ahead!

Read every book, magazine, and trade journal you can lay your hands on, so that you know what the latest buzz in the beauty industry is. Clients expect you to know about what they might have read about in an article – they look to you as the expert in the field.

The last word ...

Your head is now crammed with information and training options for a career in the beauty industry. Now major decisions need to be made to get you on the road to qualifications and success. Hopefully this book has given you an idea so that you can choose the career path that is right for you!

above: *Keep up to date with developments in the beauty industry by reading a range of publications.*

Please note that qualifications and courses are subject to change.

Publications

◎ Llewellyn, Shiona. *A Career Handbook for TV, Radio, Film, Video and Interactive Media* (A & C Black, 2003)

◎ Corson, Richard & Glavan, James. *Stage Make-Up* (Allyn & Bacon, 2001)

◎ *Hair and Beauty Studies Handbook* (HABIA/Allyn & Bacon)

◎ Taylor, Samantha. *Real Life Guide to the Beauty Industry* (Trotman, 2006)

◎ *VTCT Candidates' Handbook* (VTCT)

Careers websites

◎ City and Guilds (www.city-and-guilds.co.uk)
  – This website tells you all about City and Guilds qualifications.

◎ Connexions Direct (www.connexions-direct.com)
  – This website gives advice to young people, including learning and careers. Includes link to the Jobs4U careers database. For beauty, check out the leaflets *Working in beauty and hairdressing*, *Health and Beauty Salon*, and *Hairdressers journal*.

◎ Learndirect (www.learndirect-advice.co.uk) and Learndirect Scotland (www.learndirectscotland.com/)
  – Go to "job profiles" for details of many jobs in the beauty industry and courses and qualifications.

◎ Need2Know: Learning (www.need2know.co.uk/learning)
  – This site gives you information about study and qualifications.

◎ Qualifications and Curriculum Authority (www.qca.org.uk/14-19)
  – Go to "Qualifications" and click on "Main qualification groups" to find out about NVQs.

◎ Scottish Vocational Qualifications (www.sqa.org.uk)
  – You can find out all the latest qualifications information here.

◎ The National Council for Work Experience (www.work-experience.org/)
  – Go to "Students and Graduates" to search for placements.

Get ahead in beauty!

◎ Beauty 4 students (www.ellisons.co.uk/beauty4students)
   – This is an excellent information and resource site for students,
   including monthly treatment features.

◎ Beauty consumer (www.beautyconsumer.com)
   – You will find this site a useful reference tool. It details many
   treatments and lists the actual products that therapists use.

◎ Beautyserve (www.beautyserve.com)
   – Go to this site for information about beauty therapy, competitions,
   and exhibitions to visit.

◎ i4beauty (www.i4beauty.co.uk)
   – This website has information on beauty therapists, jobs,
   treatments, and more.

◎ The Federation of Holistic Therapists (www.fht.org.co.uk)
   – The FHT is a professional membership body that deals with
   insurance and maintaining good practice in beauty therapy.

◎ The Guild of Professional Beauty Therapists
   (www.beautyguild.com)
   – This is the trade body for professional beauty therapists in the UK.

◎ Professional beauty (www.professionalbeauty.co.uk)
   – This website gives information and dates on past and future
   exhibitions and competitions.

◎ Salon international (www.salonexhibitions.co.uk)
   – Find out about forthcoming exhibitions and trade shows
   by visiting this site.

◎ *Vitality* magazine (www.vitality-eu.com)
   – This is the website for the BABTAC magazine *Vitality*, featuring
   news and articles that have appeared in recent editions, together
   with information on advertising rates.

Useful organizations

Association of Nail Technicians

c/o Trades Exhibitions Ltd

3rd Floor, Broadway House,

2–6 Fulham Broadway

London, SW6 1AA

British Association of Beauty Therapy and Cosmetology (BABTAC)

Meteor Court, Barnett Way, Barnwood

Gloucester, GL4 3GG

(www.babtac.com)

Federation of Holistic Therapists (FHT)

3rd Floor, Eastleigh House,

Upper Market Street

Eastleigh

Hampshire, SO50 9FD

(www.fht.org.uk)

Freelance Hair and Beauty Foundation (FHBF)

The Business Centre, Kimpton Road

Luton

Bedfordshire, LU1 0LB

(www.fhbf.org.uk)

Hairdressing and Beauty Industry Authority (HABIA)

Fraser House, Nether Hall Road

Doncaster, DN1 2PH

(www.habia.org)

National Association of Screen Make-Up Artists and Hairdressers (NASMAH)

68 Sarsfield Road

Perivale

Middlesex, UB6 7AG

(www.nasmah.org.uk)

Sports Massage Association

1 Woodville Terrace, Lytham

Lancashire, FY8 5QB

(www.sportsmassageassociation.org)

The British Reflexology Association

Administration Office, Monks Orchard, Whitbourne

Worcester, WR6 5RB

(www.britreflex.co.uk)

The General Council for Massage Therapy (GCMT)

46 Millhead Way

Hertford

Herefordshire, SG14 3YH

(www.gcmt.org.uk)

The Guild of Professional Beauty Therapists (GPBT)

Guild House, 320 Burton Road

Derby, DE23 6AF

(www.beautyguild.com)

The Hairdressing Council

12 David House, 45 High Street

South Norwood

London, SE25 6HJ

(www.haircouncil.org.uk)

The International Federation of Professional Aromatherapists (IFPA)

82 Ashby Road

Hinckley

Leicestershire, LE10 1SN

(www.ifparoma.org)

accessorize decorate and beautify with the use of jewellery, scarves, handbags, for example

anatomy study of the structures of the body, for example, the muscles and bones

apprenticeship training scheme that allows you to work for money, learn, and become qualified at the same time

aromatherapy use of essential oils from flowers, herbs, and trees to help health and well-being

City and Guilds leading provider of vocational qualifications in the UK, assessing practical skills that are of use in the workplace

commission bonus paid on top of your salary. The amount of commission you earn is based on the number of goods or services you sell to clients.

competent able to do something well

complimentary therapies treatments designed to support and enhance other treatments

curriculum vitae (CV) one or two sheets of paper with information about you, your skills, and your achievements

cuticle outer layer of the hair or nail

diploma vocational qualification taken after secondary school to provide you with employment skills

dyslexic difficulty in understanding letters, numbers, symbols, and written words

electrolysis permanent hair removal using a very fine needle and mild electrical current that destroys the hair root

essential oils liquid that is taken from the leaves, stems, flowers, bark, and roots of a plant

follicle natural dip in the skin from which hair grows

freelance self-employed rather than working for a company

hazard dangerous situation that could cause harm to others

holistic treating the whole person, both mind and body, taking into account personality, lifestyle, and health

hospitality looking after visitors or guests; warmth and friendliness

incentive benefit that encourages someone to do something

intensive concentrated and demanding

interact act in such a way as to have an effect on one another

Lymphatic Drainage massage techniques used to help circulation and remove toxins (poisons) from the body

manicure nail treatment

National Vocational Qualification (NVQ) in England and Wales, a work-related, competence-based qualification that shows you have the knowledge and skills to do a job effectively. NVQs represent national standards that are recognized by employers throughout the UK

National Minimum Wage (NMW) least amount of money that can be paid to an employee

nutrition diet and good eating habits

pedicure foot treatment

perk extra advantage that you may be given when you work for a company

performance criteria things that must be assessed before you are deemed competent in a particular skill or technique

physiology study of the body's systems, for example, how the organs work

placement period of work for practical work experience as part of study

portfolio collection of work to demonstrate a person's abilities to a potential employer

probe type of needle

professional showing skill and specialized training

promotion move to a more important job with better pay

prosthetics false body parts, for example, noses, scars, and wigs

reflexology pressure massage on the feet to help relaxation and healing elsewhere in the body

Reiki healing treatment where energy from one person is passed to another

risk assessment carrying out a check of potential hazards in the work environment, to assess the likelihood of harm occurring to staff or clients

rota system by which the weekly working hours are allocated between members of staff

Scottish Vocational Qualification (SVQ) in Scotland, a work-related, competence-based qualification that shows you have the knowledge and skills to do a job effectively. SVQs represent national standards that are recognized by employers throughout the UK.

specialize become highly skilled in a particular subject or area

stamina energy and staying power

stock products which are sold to clients

Thermo-auricular Therapy use of ear candles to draw air from the ear, which helps to release pressure and relieve conditions such as allergies and headaches

tricology study and treatment of hair and scalp disorders

vocational related to the world of work and careers

Vocational Training Charitable Trust (VTCT) UK's largest awarding body for Aromatherapy, Reflexology, Massage, Holistic Therapies, and Beauty Therapy

Index

Titles in the *How to get ahead in* series include:

Hardback 978 1 4062 0442 1

Hardback 978 1 4062 0443 8

Hardback 978 1 4062 0440 7

Hardback 978 1 4062 0441 4

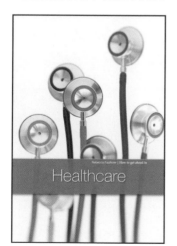

Hardback 978 1 4062 0444 5

Other titles available:

Armed and Civilian Forces	Hardback 978 1 4062 0450 6
Finance	Hardback 978 1 4062 0448 3
IT and Administration	Hardback 978 1 4062 0449 0
Leisure and Tourism	Hardback 978 1 4062 0447 6
Retail	Hardback 978 1 4062 0446 9

Find out about the other titles in this series on our website at www.raintreepublishers.co.uk